10 Minute Blocks Quilt
"Rouenneries" by French General
photo page 10
instructions pages 11-14

Florals Panel
"Essence" by Sandy Gervais
photo pages 6-7
instructions pages 15-17

Blue Skies
"Wiscasset" by Minick & Simpson
photo pages 8-9
instructions pages 18-21

Birds and Florals
"Rouenneries" by French General
photo pages 4-5
instructions pages 22-24

Peaches and Cream
"Aster Manor" by 3 Sisters
photo pages 44-45
instructions pages 25-27

Stair Steps to Heaven
"Aster Manor" by 3 Sisters
photo pages 46-47
instructions pages 28-29

Steps Around the World
"Alliance" by Howard Marcus
photo pages 48-49
instructions pages 30-33

Upstairs and Downstairs
"Rouenneries" by French General
photo pages 50-51
instructions pages 38-40

Along the Lane
"Essence" by Sandy Gervais
photo page 43
instructions pages 41-42

Birds and Florals

pieced by Rose Ann Pegram
quilted by Sue Needle

If this linen-look fabric reminds you of Colonial America or the American revolution, it is because these prints were all the rage at that time. Rouenneries are reprints of cotton fabrics produced in Rouen, France in the mid-18th century.

Capture the romance of an energetic era with the intricate prints from a golden age in textile manufacturing and enhance your decor with the clean lines of this classic design.

instructions on pages 22 - 24

"Rouenneries" by French General 'Dessert Roll' 5" strips

Florals Panel

pieced by Donna Perrotta
quilted by Sue Needle

Retro is back in fashion with a distinctive and updated sophistication.

Capture the color palette of the past in exciting patterns with this fun and deceptively easy to construct quilt.

instructions on pages 15 - 17

"Essence" by Sandy Gervais 'Jelly Roll' 2¹/₂" strips

Blue Skies

pieced by Janice Irick
quilted by Julie Lawson

Showcase your favorite printed fabric with a fast and fabulous pieced border frame. This almost 'whole cloth' quilt makes a beautiful statement in any decor.

There is surprisingly little sewing involved in this great graphic design.

instructions on pages 18 - 21

"Wiscasset" by Minick & Simpson 'Jelly Roll' $2^1/_2$" strips

10 Minute Blocks Quilt
WITH CURVED CENTERS

10 Minute Blocks Quilt
WITHOUT CURVED CENTERS

10 Minute Blocks Quilt

pieced by Donna Perrotta
quilted by Sue Needle

Create fast inset center blocks with a three seam technique. This entire quilt was pieced in a single morning. It's a great way to use up leftover squares.

Tip: The center square is perfect for showcasing fussy-cut prints, signatures of loved ones, beautiful embroidery or your favorite applique.

instructions on pages 11 - 14

"Rouenneries" by French General 'Layer Cake' 10" squares

10 Minute Blocks Quilt

photos on page 10
SIZE: 51" x 70"

YARDAGE:
We used a *Moda* "Rouenneries" by French General
 'Layer Cake' collection of 10" x 10" fabric squares
 - we purchased 1 'Layer Cake'

16 squares	OR	$1\frac{1}{6}$ yard Red
16 squares	OR	$1\frac{1}{6}$ yard Medium Gray
10 squares	OR	$\frac{7}{8}$ yard Light Gray

Border #1 & Binding   Purchase $\frac{7}{8}$ yard Red
Backing   Purchase $3\frac{1}{8}$ yards
Batting   Purchase 59" x 78"
Sewing machine, needle, thread

PREPARATION FOR SQUARES:
 Cut all squares 10" x 10".
 Label the stacks or pieces as you cut.

SORTING:
 Sort the following 10" x 10" squares into stacks:

POSITION	QUANTITY & COLOR
Block Corners	12 Red, 12 Medium Gray
Block Centers	3 Light Gray, 3 Red

MAKING THE BLOCKS:

Red Blocks -
 Make 3.
 1. For each block, choose
   4 Red background squares and 1 Light Gray square.
 Refer to the Block Construction diagrams (illustration 1).

 2. Fold a Light Gray center square 'C' in half (illustration 2).
 3. Align the raw edges of the Light Gray folded square 'C'
   with the top and right edges of a Red background square
   (illustration 3).

 Follow the steps and illustrations 4 - 14 to complete the block.
   Repeat for 2 more blocks.
   Each block will measure $19\frac{1}{2}$" x $19\frac{1}{2}$" at this point.

Gray Center Blocks -
 Make 3.
 1. For each block, choose
   4 Medium Gray background squares and 1 Red square.
 Refer to the Block Construction diagrams (illustration 1).

 2. Fold a Red center square 'C' in half (illustration 2).
 3. Align the raw edges of the Red folded square 'C'
   with the top and right edges of a Gray background square
   (illustration 3).

 Follow the steps and illustrations 4 - 14 to complete the block.
   Repeat for 2 more blocks.
   Each block will measure $19\frac{1}{2}$" x $19\frac{1}{2}$" at this point.

Block Construction Diagrams

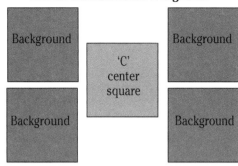

1. For each block you will need 4 background squares and 1 center 'C' square. (illustration 1)

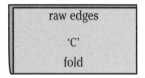

2. Fold the center square 'C' in half. (illustration 2)

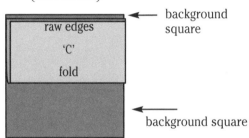

3. Align the raw edges of the folded square 'C' with the top and right edges of a background square. (illustration 3)

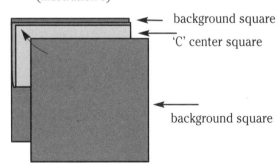

4. Sandwich the folded 'C' between the right sides of 2 background squares so the right sides are touching 'C'. (illustration 4)

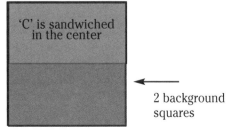

5. There should be 4 layers of fabric along the top. (illustration 5)

6. Sew a $1/4$" seam on the right side.
(illustration 6)

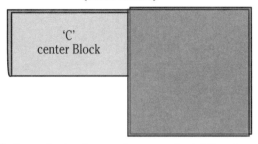

7. Open the background squares by folding them
with wrong sides together. Press.
(illustration 7)

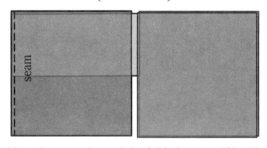

8. Align the raw edges of the folded square 'C' with
the top and left edges of a background square.

9. Sandwich the folded 'C' between the right sides of
2 background squares so the left sides are touching 'C'.

10. Sew a $1/4$" seam on the left side.
(illustration 8)

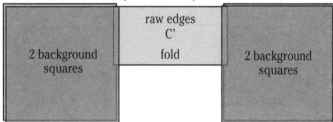

11. Open the background squares with
wrong sides together. Press.
(illustration 9)

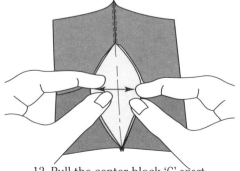

12. Pull the center block 'C' apart.
(illustration 10)

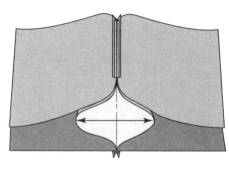

13. Flatten the seams (opening up the 'C' center
so it makes a diamond) with right sides together.
(illustration 11)

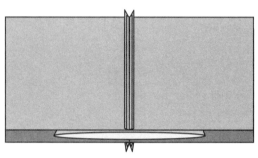

14. Pull the shape until the shape is flat.
(illustration 12)

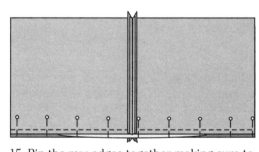

15. Pin the raw edges together making sure to
line up the seams in the center.
16. Sew a $1/4$" seam along the bottom edge.
(illustration 13)

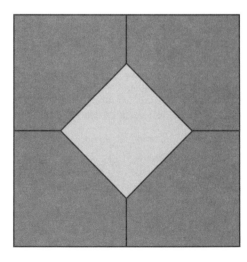

17. Open the piece and pull the shape until it is flat
and the 'C' center forms a layered diamond. Press.
(illustration 14)

Terrific Tips:

At this point you have options:

1.) Topstitch along edges of center square with decorative thread.

2.) Gently pull the edge toward the center of the block forming a curve like a 'Cathedral Window' design. Topstitch or Blind Hem stitch the curves in place.

3.) Embroider a design or save this space for a decorative quilting motif.

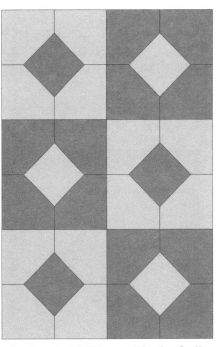

Option 1:
Quilt with Square Blocks in the Center

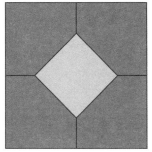

Square Blocks in the Center
Make 6

Topstitch along the edges of each block to hold the edges down flat.

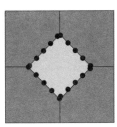

Or Topstitch along the edges of each block with a decorative stitch

Option 1: 10 Minute Blocks Quilt with Square Blocks in the Center
Quilt Assembly Diagram

ASSEMBLY:
Arrange all blocks on a work surface or table.
Refer to diagram for block placement.
Sew blocks together in 3 rows, 2 blocks per row. Press.
Sew the rows together.Press.

Option 2:
Quilt with Curved Blocks in the Center

Cathedral Window

Create interesting 'Cathedral Window' style curves in the center of each large block. This technique is simple and creates a wonderfully mysterious look.

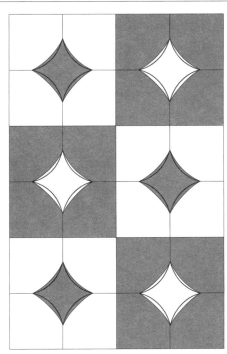

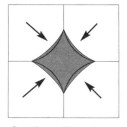

Gently pull the loose edge of each side of the center square toward the center of the block forming a curve.

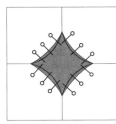

Pin in place. Topstitch along the edges of each block to hold the edges down flat.

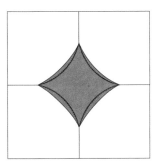

Curved Blocks in the Center
Make 6

Option 2: 10 Minute Blocks Quilt with Curved Blocks in the Center
Quilt Assembly Diagram

ASSEMBLY:
Arrange all blocks on a work surface or table.
Refer to diagram for block placement.
Sew blocks together in 3 rows, 2 blocks per row. Press.
Sew the rows together.Press.

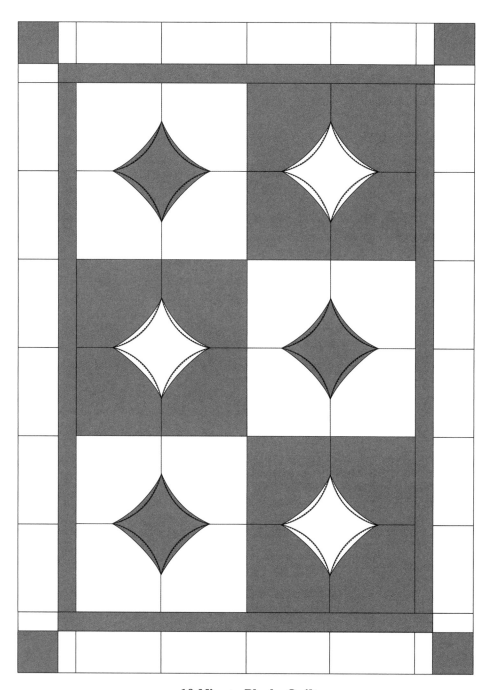

10 Minute Blocks Quilt

Add the Borders
Quilt Assembly Diagram

BORDERS:

for Quilts with Square Blocks and
for Quilts with Curved Block

Border #1:
Cut 2 strips $2\frac{1}{2}$" x $57\frac{1}{2}$" for sides.
Cut 2 strips $2\frac{1}{2}$" x $42\frac{1}{2}$" for top
    and bottom.
Sew side borders to the quilt.
    Press.
Sew top and bottom borders to
    the quilt. Press.

Pieced Border #2:
Cut 1 Light Gray square into
    8 strips, each $2\frac{1}{2}$" x 5".
Cut 6 Light Gray squares into
    12 rectangles, each 5" x 10".
Cut 4 Dark Gray squares into
    8 rectangles, each 5" x 10".
Cut 1 Red square into
    4 cornerstones, each 5" x 5".

Side Borders:
Sew
        a Light Gray strip,
        6 rectangles, and
        a Light Gray strip to
    to make a piece $4\frac{1}{2}$" x $61\frac{1}{2}$".
        Make 2.
    Sew side borders to the quilt.
        Press.

Top and Bottom Borders:
Sew
        a Red cornerstone,
        Light Gray strip,
        4 rectangles,
        a Light Gray strip and
        a Red cornerstone
    to make a piece $4\frac{1}{2}$" x $51\frac{1}{2}$".
        Make 2.
    Sew top and bottom borders to
        the quilt. Press.

FINISHING:
Quilting:
See Basic Instructions.
Binding:
Cut strips $2\frac{1}{2}$" wide.
Sew together end to end to equal 252".

See Binding Instructions.

Florals Panel

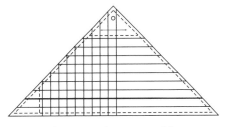

photos on pages 6 - 7
SIZE: 54" x 75"

YARDAGE:
We used a *Moda* "Essence" by Sandy Gervais
   'Jelly Roll' collection of $2\frac{1}{2}$" strips
   - we purchased 1 'Jelly Roll'

6 strips	OR	$\frac{1}{2}$ yard Cream
6 strips	OR	$\frac{1}{2}$ yard Brown
6 strips	OR	$\frac{1}{2}$ yard Teal
3 strips	OR	$\frac{1}{4}$ yard Red
3 strips	OR	$\frac{1}{4}$ yard Gold

Center Panel   Purchase $1\frac{1}{4}$ yards of printed
                            fabric or a printed panel for the center
Cornerstones   Purchase $\frac{5}{8}$ yard Teal
Border #2 & Binding   Purchase $1\frac{7}{8}$ yards Cream print
Backing   Purchase $3\frac{3}{8}$ yards
Batting   Purchase 62" x 83"
Sewing machine, needle, thread
Plastic Template:
   Fons & Porter (Omnigrid) 'Easy Diagonal Sets' Ruler

See triangle on page 19

PREPARATION FOR STRIPS:
   Cut all strips $2\frac{1}{2}$" x width of
      fabric (usually 42" - 44").

SORTING:
   Group 3 sets of 8 strips for
      making strip sets.

CENTER PANEL:
   Cut a printed fabric or panel
      to $21\frac{1}{2}$" x $42\frac{1}{2}$".

CORNERSTONES:
   Cut 4 Teal print squares,
      each 11" x 11".

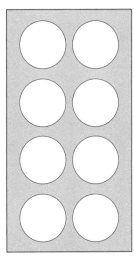

Center Panel
$21\frac{1}{2}$" x $42\frac{1}{2}$"

Cornerstones
Cut 4
11" x 11".

MAKING THE BLOCKS
FOR PIECED BORDER #1:

Cream
Red
Teal
Brown
Teal
Brown
Cream
Gold

Strip Sets
Sew 8 strips together following the color suggestion above.
   Note: This color selection will create an interesting design
      with lighter colors on the top and left of the quilt and
      darker colors on the bottom and right of the quilt.
   Make 3 strip sets.

Sew a $\frac{1}{4}$" seam

fold

Form a 'Tube'
   With right sides together, fold each strip set in half
      lengthwise to form a 'tube'.
   Sew a $\frac{1}{4}$" seam across the top.

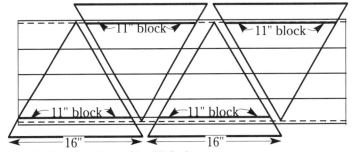

11" block   11" block
11" block   11" block
16"   16"

Cut Triangles from the 'Tube'
   Align the 11" block line of the ruler with the bottom
      seam (not the edge).
   Cut a triangle block.

   Turn the ruler upside down and align the 11" block ruler
      mark with the top seam (not the edge).
   Cut another triangle block.

   Repeat, cutting 4 triangle blocks from each strip set for a
      total of 12 triangle blocks.

Triangle Blocks are Square Blocks
Unfold each triangle to form a square. Press.
   Trim each square to 11" x 11".
   Note: You will have 2 styles of blocks.

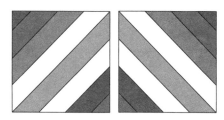

Position blocks

Sew 2 blocks for the top border.

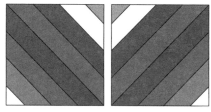

Position blocks

Sew 2 blocks for the bottom border.

SEW BLOCKS TOGETHER:
Top and Bottom Borders:
Sew blocks together in pairs to make
the border strips.

Sew 2 blocks together for the
top and bottom.

Make 2 (1 set of light and
1 set of dark).

Side Borders:
Sew 4 blocks together for each side.

Make 2 (1 set of light and
1 set of dark).

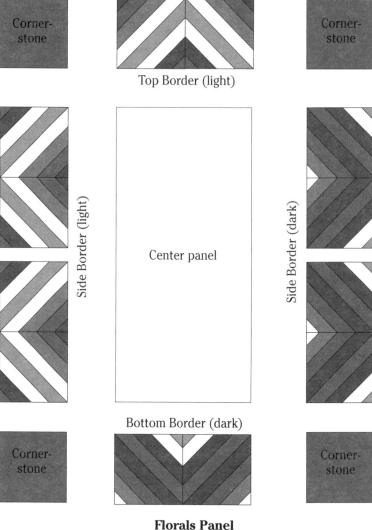

Florals Panel
Quilt Assembly Diagram

ASSEMBLY:
Refer to Quilt Assembly diagram for block placement.
Arrange all blocks on a work surface or table.

BORDERS:
Side Border Strips:
Sew 4 blocks to make a piece 11" x 42$\frac{1}{2}$". Press.
Make 2.
Sew to the sides of the Center panel. Press.
Top and Bottom Border Strips:
Sew a Cornerstone - 2 blocks - a Cornerstone
to make a piece 11" x 42$\frac{1}{2}$". Press.
Make 2.
Sew to the top and bottom of the Center panel. Press.

Florals Panel
Quilt Assembly Diagram

Outer Border #2:
Cut strips $6\frac{1}{2}$" wide parallel to the selvage to
      eliminate piecing.
      Cut 2 strips $6\frac{1}{2}$" x $63\frac{1}{2}$" for sides.
      Cut 2 strips $6\frac{1}{2}$" x $54\frac{1}{2}$" for top and bottom.
      Sew side borders to the quilt. Press.
      Sew top and bottom borders to the quilt. Press.

FINISHING:
Quilting: See Basic Instructions.
Binding: Cut strips $2\frac{1}{2}$" wide.
      Sew together end to end to equal 268".
      See Binding Instructions.

Blue Skies

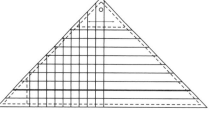

photos on pages 8 - 9
SIZE: 60" x 76"

See triangle on page 19

YARDAGE:
We used a *Moda* "Wiscasset" by Minick & Simpson
    'Jelly Roll' collection of $2\frac{1}{2}$" strips
    - we purchased 1 'Jelly Roll'

11 strips	OR	$\frac{7}{8}$ yard Blue
12 strips	OR	$\frac{7}{8}$ yard Tan/Cream
5 strips	OR	$\frac{3}{8}$ yard Red

Center Panel   Purchase $1\frac{3}{8}$ yards Blue print
Border & Binding   Purchase $1\frac{7}{8}$ yards Blue print
Backing   Purchase $3\frac{7}{8}$ yards
Batting   Purchase 68" x 84"
Sewing machine, needle, thread
Plastic Template:
    Fons & Porter (Omnigrid) 'Easy Diagonal Sets' ruler

QUILT CENTER:
Cut a large whole
cloth panel
for the center.
We used a Blue print
$32\frac{1}{2}$" x $48\frac{1}{2}$".

Center Panel
Cut a whole cloth piece
$32\frac{1}{2}$" x $48\frac{1}{2}$"

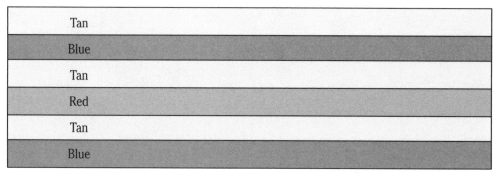

MAKE THE BLOCKS:
Strip Sets
Sew 6 strips together to make a piece $12\frac{1}{2}$" x 42".
    Follow the color suggestion above, Tan-Blue-Tan-Red-Tan-Blue. Press. Make 4 strip sets.

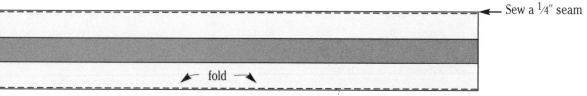

← Sew a $\frac{1}{4}$" seam

fold

Form a 'Tube'
    With right sides together, fold each strip set in half lengthwise to form a 'tube'.
    Sew a $\frac{1}{4}$" seam across the top.

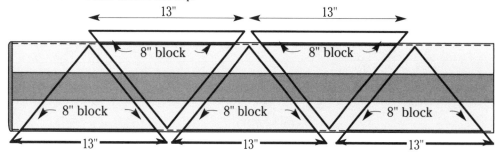

Cut Triangles from the 'Tubes'
    Align the 8" block line of the ruler with the bottom seam (not the edge).
        Cut a triangle block.
    Turn the ruler upside down and align the 8" block ruler mark with the top seam (not the edge).
        Cut another triangle block.
    Repeat, cutting 5 triangle blocks from each strip set for a total of 20 squares, each $8\frac{1}{2}$" x $8\frac{1}{2}$".

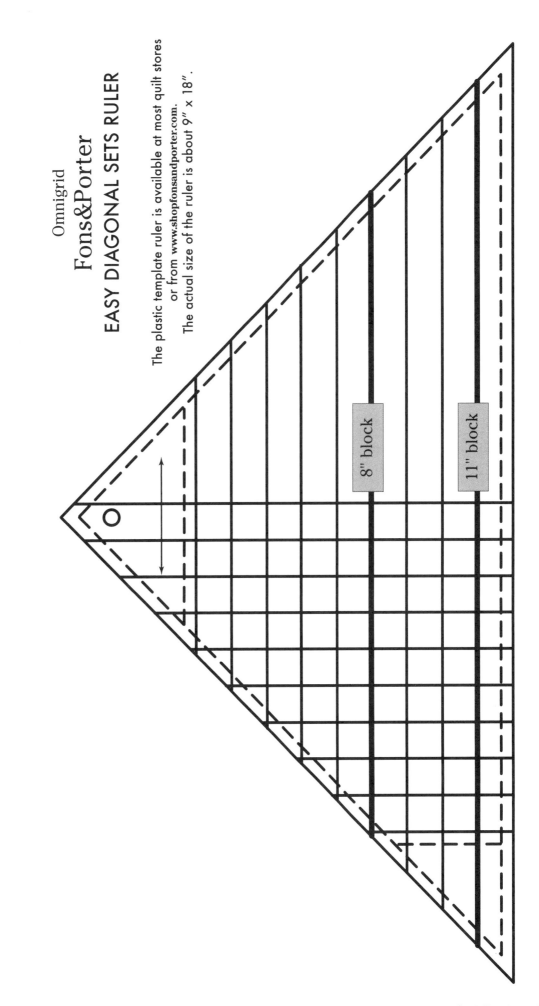

Omnigrid
Fons&Porter
EASY DIAGONAL SETS RULER

The plastic template ruler is available at most quilt stores
or from www.shopfonsandporter.com.
The actual size of the ruler is about 9" x 18".

O

8" block

11" block

Square Blocks

Unfold each triangle block to form a square.
   Press.
Center & trim each square to $8\frac{1}{2}$" x $8\frac{1}{2}$".
Note: You will have 2 styles of blocks.

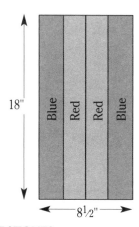

18"

Blue | Red | Red | Blue

$8\frac{1}{2}$"

CORNERSTONES:
Cornerstone Center

Cut 2 Blue and 2 Red strips, each 18" long.
Sew strips together: B-R-R-B to make a piece
   $8\frac{1}{2}$" x 18". Press.

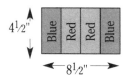

$4\frac{1}{2}$"

Blue | Red | Red | Blue

$8\frac{1}{2}$"

Center Section

Cut the piece into 4 sections for the center,
   each $4\frac{1}{2}$" x $8\frac{1}{2}$".

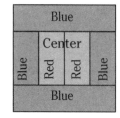

Blue
Center
Blue | Red | Red | Blue
Blue

Cornerstone Assembly

Cut 8 Blue strips, each $8\frac{1}{2}$" long.

Sew a Blue strip to the top and bottom of
   each Center section.
   Press.
Make 4 Cornerstone squares.

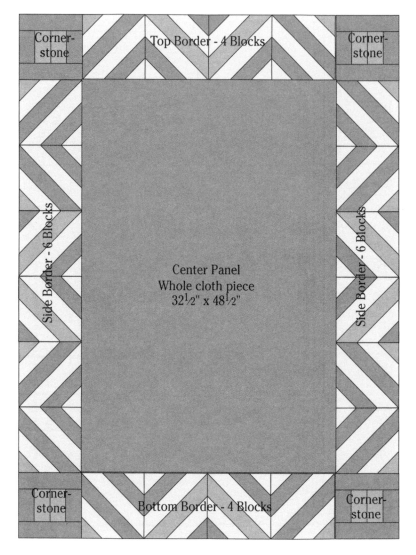

Blue Skies
Quilt Assembly Diagram

ASSEMBLY:
   Arrange all blocks on a work surface or table.

Pieced Border #1:
   Sides:
   Sew 6 border squares together to make a section $8\frac{1}{2}$" x $48\frac{1}{2}$".
      Press. Make 2.
   Sew side borders to the quilt center. Press.

   Top and Bottom:
   Sew 4 border squares together to make a section $8\frac{1}{2}$" x $32\frac{1}{2}$".
      Press. Make 2.
   Sew a Cornerstone to each end. Press.
   Sew top and bottom borders to the quilt center. Press.

Blue Skies
Quilt Assembly Diagram

BORDERS:

Outer Border #2:
Cut strips $6\frac{1}{2}$" wide parallel to the selvage to
   eliminate piecing.
   Cut 2 strips $6\frac{1}{2}$" x $64\frac{1}{2}$" for sides.
   Cut 2 strips $6\frac{1}{2}$" x $60\frac{1}{2}$" for top and bottom.
   Sew side borders to the quilt. Press.
   Sew top and bottom borders to the quilt.
      Press.

FINISHING:
Quilting: See Basic Instructions.
Binding: Cut strips $2\frac{1}{2}$" wide.
      Sew together end to end to equal 282".
      See Binding Instructions.

Birds and Florals

photos on pages 4 - 5
SIZE: 68" x 92"

YARDAGE:

We used a *Moda* "Rouenneries" by French General
    'Dessert Roll' collection of 5" x 44" fabric strips
    - we purchased 1 'Dessert Roll'
    2 strips, 5" x 44"   OR $\frac{1}{3}$ yard Dark Red
    2 strips, 5" x 44"   OR $\frac{1}{3}$ yard Light Red
    2 strips, 5" x 44"   OR $\frac{1}{3}$ yard Tan
    2 strips, 5" x 44"   OR $\frac{1}{3}$ yard Ivory

Center block   Purchase 2 yards of Ivory print
Border #1   Purchase $\frac{1}{2}$ yard Red print
Border #3 & Binding   Purchase $2\frac{1}{4}$ yards Red print
Backing   Purchase $5\frac{5}{8}$ yards
Batting   Purchase 76" x 100"
Sewing machine, needle, thread

PREPARATION FOR STRIPS:

Cut all strips 5" x width of fabric (usually 42" - 44").

QUILT CENTER:

Cut a whole cloth piece for the center block $44\frac{1}{2}$" x $68\frac{1}{2}$".

Quilt Center
Cut a whole cloth piece
$44\frac{1}{2}$" x $68\frac{1}{2}$".

QUILT CENTER:

Cut a whole cloth piece $44\frac{1}{2}$" x $68\frac{1}{2}$" for the center block.

HALF-SQUARE TRIANGLES:

Pair up and Cut Dark Squares:
    Pair up a Dark Red 5" strip
with a Tan 5" strip, with right sides
together.

    Cut each pair of strips into 8
squares, each 5" x 5" for a total of
16 squares (8 pair).

    Repeat once for a total
of 32 squares (16 pair).

Pair up and Cut Light Squares:
    Repeat with 2 pair of Light Red
and Ivory 5" strips for a total of
32 more squares (16 pair).

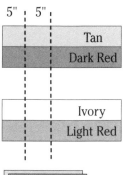

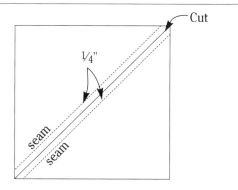

Half-Square Triangle

1. Place 2 squares right sides together.
2. Draw a diagonal line from corner to corner.
3. Stitch $\frac{1}{4}$" on each side of the line.
4. Cut squares apart on the diagonal line.
5. Open the 2 new squares with 2 colors.
6. Press. Trim off dog-ears.
7. Center and trim to size.

Sew and Cut into Half Square Triangles:
Follow the instructions in the
    Half-Square Triangle diagram to
    sew and cut squares diagonally
    to make 64 half-square triangles.

    Trim each block to $4\frac{1}{2}$" x $4\frac{1}{2}$".

Each pair of squares will make 2 Half-Square Triangle blocks.

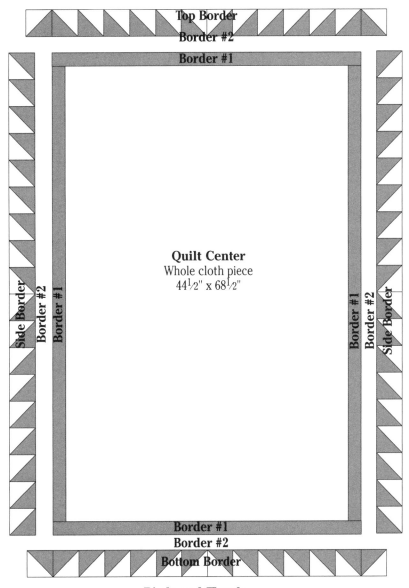

Birds and Florals
Quilt Assembly Diagram

BORDERS:
Border #1:
   Cut 2 strips $2^1/2$" x $68^1/2$" for sides.
   Cut 2 strips $2^1/2$" x $48^1/2$" for top and bottom.
   Sew side borders to the quilt. Press.
   Sew top and bottom borders to the quilt. Press.

Half-Square Triangle Border #2:
   You will need a total of 64 Half-Square Triangle blocks.
   Arrange all half-square triangles on a work surface or table.
   Refer to diagram for block placement.

   Side Borders:
      Sew a strip of 18 half-square triangles to make a piece $4^1/2$" x $72^1/2$".
         Press. Make 2.
         Note: Be sure the triangles are positioned like the illustration above.
      Sew side borders to the quilt. Press.

   Top and Bottom Borders:
      Sew a strip of 14 half-square triangles to make a piece $4^1/2$" x $56^1/2$".
         Press. Make 2.
         Note: Be sure the triangles are positioned like the illustration above,
         especially the corner squares.
   Sew top and bottom borders to the quilt. Press.

Birds and Florals
Quilt Assembly Diagram

Outer Border #3:
Cut strips $6\frac{1}{2}$" wide parallel to the selvage to
    eliminate piecing.
    Cut 2 strips $6\frac{1}{2}$" x $80\frac{1}{2}$" for sides.
    Cut 2 strips $6\frac{1}{2}$" x $68\frac{1}{2}$" for top and bottom.
    Sew side borders to the quilt. Press.
    Sew top and bottom borders to the quilt. Press.

FINISHING:
Quilting: See Basic Instructions.

Binding: Cut strips $2\frac{1}{2}$" wide.
    Sew together end to end to equal 330".
    See Binding Instructions.

Peaches and Cream

photos on pages 44 - 45
SIZE: $52\frac{1}{2}$" x $70\frac{1}{2}$"

YARDAGE:
We used a *Moda* "Aster Manor" by 3 Sisters
   'Dessert Roll' collection of 5" x 44" fabric strips
   - we purchased 1 'Dessert Roll'

3 strips	OR	$\frac{1}{2}$ yard Red
3 strips	OR	$\frac{1}{2}$ yard Cream
2 strips	OR	$\frac{1}{3}$ yard Gold
1 strip	OR	$\frac{1}{6}$ yard Peach

Blocks	Purchase $\frac{1}{2}$ yard Pink medium print
Border #1 & Blocks	Purchase $\frac{2}{3}$ yard Cream small print
Border #2 & Binding	Purchase $1\frac{7}{8}$ yard Pink large print
Backing	Purchase $3\frac{1}{3}$ yards
Batting	Purchase 61" x 79"
Sewing machine, needle, thread	

PREPARATION FOR STRIPS:
   Cut all strips 5" x width of fabric (usually 42" - 44").

CUTTING:

CUT 5" STRIPS FROM YARDAGE:

	Quantity	Length	Position by Row Number
Pink medium print	3	5" x width of fabric	
		Then cut the following pieces:	
	9	5" x 14"	#1, 2, 4, 5, 7, 8, 10, 11, 13
Cream small print:	2	5" x width of fabric	
		Then cut the following pieces:	
	3	5" x 14"	#3, 6, 11
	3	5" x $7\frac{1}{4}$"	#4, 8, 12

CUT 5" DESSERT ROLL STRIPS:

	Quantity	Length	Position by Row Number
Red	7	14"	#1, 3, 6, 9, 10, 12, 13
	2	$7\frac{1}{4}$"	#2, 8
Cream	6	14"	#2, 4, 5, 7, 8, 12
	5	$7\frac{1}{4}$"	#4, 6, 6, 10, 10
Gold	6	14"	#1, 3, 7, 9, 11, 13
Peach	2	14"	#5, 9
	2	$7\frac{1}{4}$"	#2, 12

ASSEMBLY:
   Refer to Quilt Assembly diagram on page 26.
   Arrange all blocks on a work surface or table.

Making Rows
   Sew blocks together for each row (3 or 4 blocks per row).
   Note: There are 3 blocks on rows 1, 3, 5, 7, 9, 11 and 13.
   Note: There are 4 blocks on rows 2, 4, 6, 8, 10 and 12.
   Press each row.

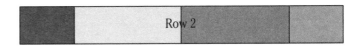

Sew Rows
   Sew the rows together (a total of 13 rows).
     Press.

Row 1	Medium Print	Red	Gold
Row 2	Red	Cream	Medium Print	Peach
Row 3	Small Print	Gold	Red
Row 4	Cream	Medium Print	Cream	Small Print
Row 5	Peach	Cream	Medium Print
Row 6	Cream	Red	Small Print	Cream
Row 7	Medium Print	Cream	Gold
Row 8	Small Print	Cream	Medium Print	Red
Row 9	Red	Gold	Peach
Row 10	Cream	Medium Print	Red	Cream
Row 11	Gold	Small Print	Medium Print
Row 12	Peach	Red	Cream	Small Print
Row 13	Medium Print	Gold	Red

Peaches and Cream
Quilt Assembly Diagram

Peaches and Cream
Quilt Assembly Diagram

BORDERS:
Border #1:
    Cut 2 strips $2\frac{1}{2}$" x 41" for top and bottom.
    Cut 2 strips $2\frac{1}{2}$" x 63" for sides.
    Sew top and bottom borders to the quilt. Press.
    Sew side borders to the quilt. Press.

Outer Border #2:
Cut strips $4\frac{1}{2}$" wide parallel to the selvage to eliminate piecing.
    Cut 2 strips $4\frac{1}{2}$" x 63" for sides.
    Cut 2 strips $4\frac{1}{2}$" x 53" for top and bottom.
    Sew side borders to the quilt. Press.
    Sew top and bottom borders to the quilt. Press.

FINISHING:
Quilting:
    See Basic Instructions.
Binding:
    Cut strips $2\frac{1}{2}$" wide.
    Sew together end to end to equal 258".
    See Binding Instructions.

Stair Steps to Heaven

photos on pages 46 - 47
SIZE: 63½" x 76¾"

YARDAGE:
We used a *Moda* "Aster Manor" by 3 Sisters
  'Layer Cake' collection of 10" x 10" squares
  - we purchased 1 'Layer Cake'

9 squares	OR	⅞ yard Brown
7 squares	OR	⅝ yard Cream
6 squares	OR	⅝ yard Red
6 squares	OR	⅝ yard Pink
6 squares	OR	⅝ yard Tan

Border #1	Purchase ½ yard Brown
Border #2 & Binding	Purchase 1⅞ yards Brown floral
Backing	Purchase 4 yards
Batting	Purchase 72" x 85"

Sewing machine, needle, thread

PREPARATION FOR SQUARES:
  To get started, cut all squares 10" x 10".

CUTTING:

Cut Brown Strips:
  Use 9 Brown squares.
  Cut each square into 3 strips, each 3¼" x 10".
  You will need 25 strips.

Cut Cream Strips and Sections:
  Use 2 Cream squares.
  Cut each square into 1 strip 3¼" x 10"
    and 1 section 6¾" x 10".

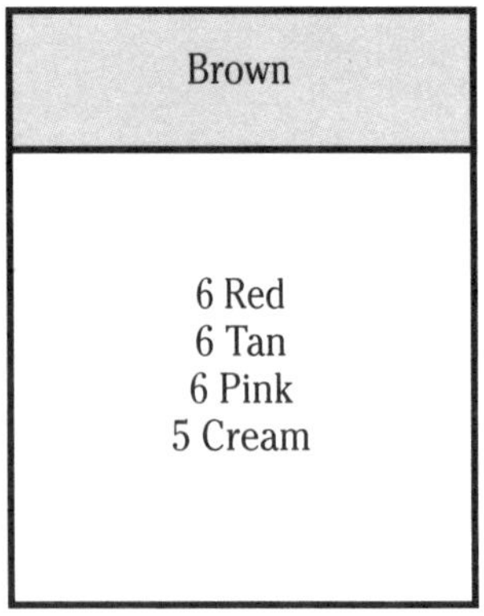

Brown
6 Red 6 Tan 6 Pink 5 Cream

Block A
10" x 12¾". Make 23.

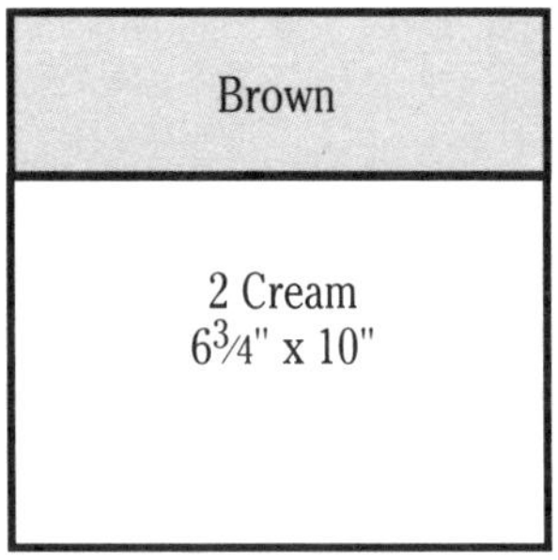

Brown
2 Cream 6¾" x 10"

Block B
10" x 9½". Make 2.

MAKING THE BLOCKS:

Block A:
  You need the following 10" squares:
    6 Red, 6 Tan, 6 Pink, 5 Cream.
  Sew a Brown strip to the top of each 10" square. Press.
  Each block will measure 10" x 12¾".
  Make 23.

Block B:
  Sew a Brown strip to the top of each Cream 6¾" x 10"
    strip. Press. Each block will measure 9½" x 10".
  Make 2.

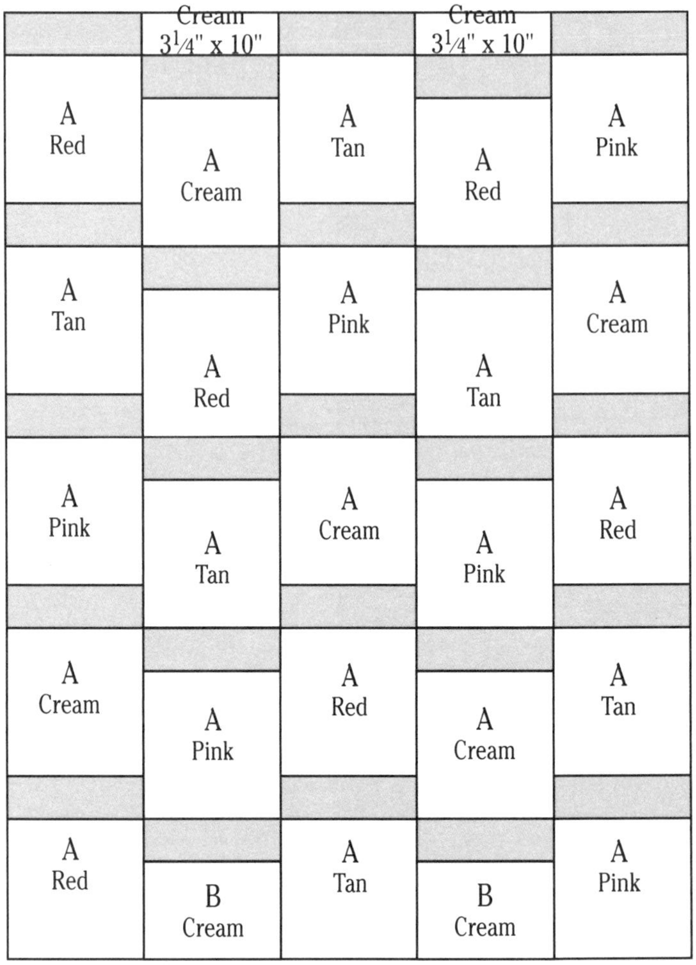

Col 1	Col 2	Col 3	Col 4	Col 5
	Cream 3¼" x 10"		Cream 3¼" x 10"	
A Red	A Cream	A Tan	A Red	A Pink
A Tan	A Red	A Pink	A Tan	A Cream
A Pink	A Tan	A Cream	A Pink	A Red
A Cream	A Pink	A Red	A Cream	A Tan
A Red	B Cream	A Tan	B Cream	A Pink

Stair Steps to Heaven
Quilt Assembly Diagram

ASSEMBLY:
  Arrange all blocks on a work surface or table.
  Refer to diagram for block placement.

Column 1:
  Sew Red-Tan-Pink-Cream-Red. Press.

Column 2:
  Sew Cream-Red-Tan-Pink-Block B. Press.
  Sew a Cream 3¼" x 10" strip to the top of the row. Press.

Column 3:
  Sew Tan-Pink-Cream-Red-Tan. Press.

Column 4:
  Sew Red-Tan-Pink-Cream-Block B. Press.
  Sew a Cream 3¼" x 10" strip to the top of the row. Press.

Column 5:
  Sew Pink-Cream-Red-Tan-Pink. Press.
  Columns 1, 3 & 5 are ½" longer than columns 2 & 4.
  Align the tops of the columns and match the seams.
  Sew the columns together. Press.
  Trim the bottom of the quilt even.

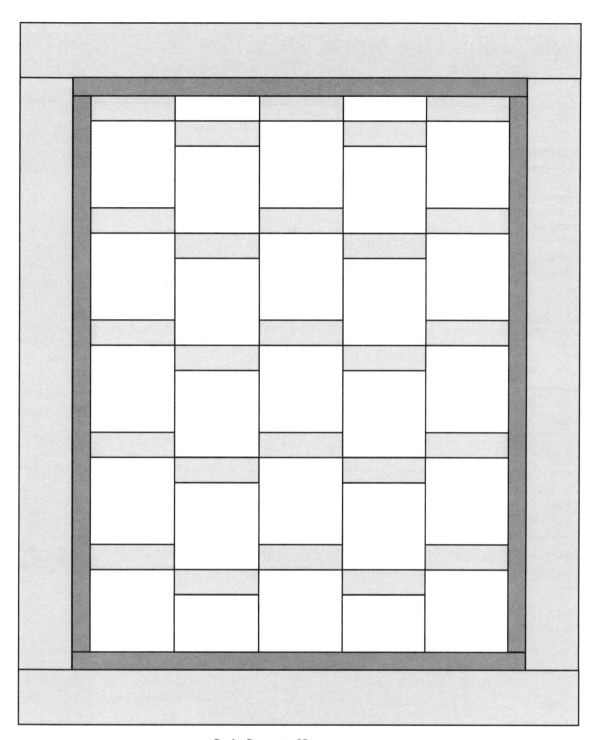

Stair Steps to Heaven
Quilt Assembly Diagram

BORDERS:
Border #1:
    Cut 2 strips $2\frac{1}{2}$" x $61\frac{1}{4}$" for sides.
    Cut 2 strips $2\frac{1}{2}$" x 52" for top and bottom.
    Sew side borders to the quilt. Press.
    Sew top and bottom borders to the quilt. Press.

Outer Border #2:
Cut strips $6\frac{1}{2}$" wide parallel to the selvage to
      eliminate piecing.
    Cut 2 strips $6\frac{1}{2}$" x $65\frac{1}{4}$" for sides.
    Cut 2 strips $6\frac{1}{2}$" x 64" for top and bottom.
    Sew side borders to the quilt. Press.
    Sew top and bottom borders to the quilt. Press.

FINISHING:
Quilting: See Basic Instructions.
Binding: Cut strips $2\frac{1}{2}$" wide.
      Sew together end to end to equal 291".
      See Binding Instructions.

Steps Around the World

photos on pages 49 - 49
SIZE: 67" x 87"

YARDAGE:

We used a *Moda* "Alliance" by Howard Marcus
'Layer Cake' collection of 10" x 10" squares
- we purchased 1 'Layer Cake'

10 squares	OR	$^7/8$ yard Light Brown
10 squares	OR	$^7/8$ yard Dark Brown
4 squares	OR	$^1/3$ yard Blue

Border #1	Purchase $^1/4$ yard Brown
Border #2 & Sashing	Purchase $^2/3$ yard Red
Center, Border #4 & Binding	Purchase 3 yards Dark Red
Backing	Purchase $5^1/2$ yards
Batting	Purchase 75" x 95"

Sewing machine, needle, thread

PREPARATION FOR SQUARES:

Cut all squares 10" x 10".
Label the stacks or pieces as you cut.

SORTING:

Sort the following 10" x 10" squares into stacks:

position	quantity	color
Blue	4	Cornerstones
Light Brown	10	Half-Square Triangles
Dark Brown	10	Half-Square Triangles

CENTER:

Cut Dark Red yardage
to $36^1/2$" x $56^1/2$".

HALF-SQUARE TRIANGLES:
Pair up Squares:
Pair up a Light Brown
10" square with a
Dark Brown 10" square,
with right sides together.

Repeat 9 times more for a total
of 10 pair of squares.

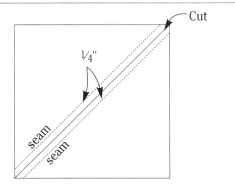

Half-Square Triangle

1. Place 2 squares right sides together.
2. Draw a diagonal line from corner to corner.
3. Stitch $^1/4$" on each side of the line.
4. Cut squares apart on the diagonal line.
5. Open the 2 new squares with 2 colors.
6. Press. Trim off dog-ears.
7. Center and trim to size.

Sew and Cut into
Half Square Triangles:

Follow the instructions in
the Half-Square Triangle
diagram to sew and
cut squares diagonally
to make 20
half-square triangles.
Trim each block to
$9^1/2$" x $9^1/2$".

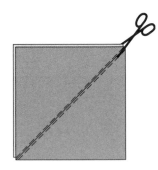

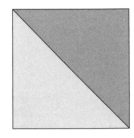

Each pair of squares will make 2 Half-Square Triangle blocks
for a total of 20 blocks.

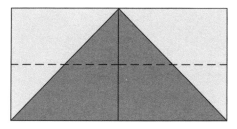

PIECED BORDER #3

Sew Blocks Together

1. Pair up 2 matching Half Square Triangles and sew them together in the center to make $9\frac{1}{2}$" x $18\frac{1}{2}$". Press.

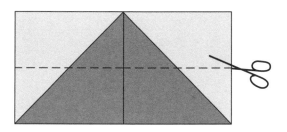

Cut Blocks in Half Horizontally

2. Cut each pair of Half-Square Triangles in half horizontally, each $4\frac{3}{4}$" x $18\frac{1}{2}$".

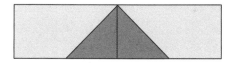

Sections

3. You will have 2 sections, each $4\frac{3}{4}$" x $18\frac{1}{2}$".

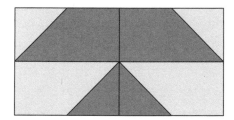

Sew the Sections Together

4. Sew the rectangular sections together to make 9" x $18\frac{1}{2}$". Press.
Make a total of 10 blocks.

SASHING:

Sashing:
   Cut 14 Red $2\frac{1}{2}$" x 9" strips.

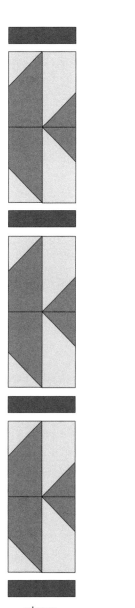

pieces

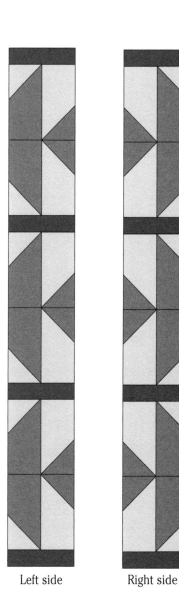

Left side   Right side

PIECED SIDE BORDERS

5. Lay sections out on a work surface or table to choose positions for the colors of sections.
6. Position side border sections in 2 columns, 3 rectangles per row with 4 strips.
   Sew a strip-block-strip-block-strip-block-strip to make a piece 9" x $62\frac{1}{2}$".
   Make 2. Press.
   Turn 1 section for the left side and 1 section for the right side.

CORNERSTONES:
Cut 4 Blue squares, each 9" x 9".

Top border

Bottom border

PIECED TOP AND BOTTOM BORDERS
7. Lay sections out on a work surface or table to choose positions for the colors.
8. Position sections in 2 rows,
      2 cornerstones and 2 rectangles per row with 3 strips.
   Sew a cornerstone-strip-block-strip-block-strip-cornerstone
      to make a piece 9" x 59$\frac{1}{2}$".
   Make 2. Press.
   Turn 1 for the top border and 1 for the bottom border.

BROWN BORDER #1:
      Cut 2 strips 1$\frac{1}{2}$" x 56$\frac{1}{2}$" for sides.
      Cut 2 strips 1$\frac{1}{2}$" x 38$\frac{1}{2}$" for top and bottom.

      Sew side borders to the center. Press.
      Sew top and bottom borders to the quilt. Press.

RED BORDER #2:
      Cut 2 strips 2$\frac{1}{2}$" x 58$\frac{1}{2}$" for sides.
      Cut 2 strips 2$\frac{1}{2}$" x 42$\frac{1}{2}$" for top and bottom.

      Sew side borders to the quilt. Press.
      Sew top and bottom borders to the quilt. Press.

PIECED BORDER #3:
      Sew side borders to the quilt. Press.
      Sew top and bottom borders to the quilt. Press.

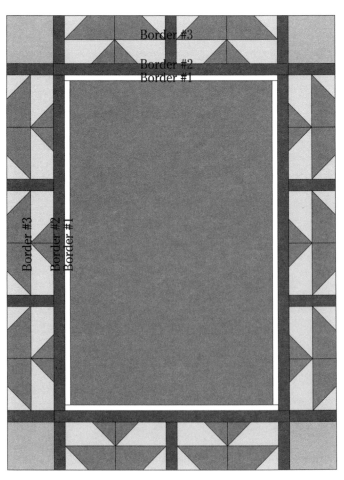

Steps Around the World
Quilt Assembly Diagram

Steps Around the World
Quilt Assembly Diagram

OUTER BORDER #4:
Cut strips $4\frac{1}{2}$" x the width of fabric. Sew strips
    together end to end.
    Cut 2 strips $4\frac{1}{2}$" x $79\frac{1}{2}$" for sides.
    Cut 2 strips $4\frac{1}{2}$" x $67\frac{1}{2}$" for top and bottom.

Sew side borders to the quilt. Press.
Sew top and bottom borders to the quilt. Press.

FINISHING:
Quilting: See Basic Instructions.

Binding: Cut strips $2\frac{1}{2}$" wide.
        Sew together end to end to equal 318".
        See Binding Instructions

The Best Things About
'Jelly Rolls' – 'Dessert Rolls' – 'Layer Cakes'

I love to quilt, but it is often difficult to find time to cut and piece a quilt top. When I saw collections of 2^1/$_2$" pre-cut fabric strips, 5" pre-cut strips and the selections of 10" pre-cut squares, I knew they were the answer.

No more spending hours choosing and cutting fabrics. Now I can begin sewing right away. Beautiful colors are available in every set. So whether I like jewel colors, heritage patterns, soft pastels or earthy tones... there is an assortment for me.

Now my goals... a handmade cover for every bed, an heirloom quilt for each new baby and a pieced quilt for each of my children... are within reach. With 'Jelly Rolls', 'Dessert Rolls' and 'Layer Cakes' it is possible to complete a quilt top in a weekend.

After I piece all the blocks together, I use leftover strips for the borders and binding. Nothing really goes to waste and, if needed, I can purchase a bit of extra fabric for an extra punch of color or an additional yard for the border.

TIP: Quantities are given in strips or squares and yardage so you know what you need and can start right away.

Tips for Working with Strips

Guide for Yardage:

2^1/$_2$" Strips - Each ¼ yard or a 'Fat Quarter' equals 3 strips - A pre-cut 'Jelly Roll' strip is 2½" x 44"

5" Strips - Each ⅓ yard equals 2 strips - A pre-cut 'Dessert Roll' strip is 5" x 44"

10" x 10" Squares - Four 10" squares can be cut from ⅓ yard or eight 10" squares can be cut from ⅝ yard.

Pre-cut strips are cut on the crosswise grain and are prone to stretching. These tips will help reduce stretching and make your quilt lay flat for quilting.

1. If you are cutting yardage, cut on the grain. Cut fat quarters on grain, parallel to the 18" side.

2. When sewing crosswise grain strips together, take care not to stretch the strips. If you detect any puckering as you go, rip out the seam and sew it again.

3. Press, Do Not Iron. Carefully open fabric, with the seam to one side, press without moving the iron. A back-and-forth ironing motion stretches the fabric.

4. Reduce the wiggle in your borders with this technique from garment making. First, accurately cut your borders to the exact measure of the quilt top. Then, before sewing the border to the quilt, run a double row of stay stitches along the outside edge to maintain the original shape and prevent stretching. Pin the border to the quilt, taking care not to stretch the quilt top to make it fit. Pinning reduces slipping and stretching.

Rotary Cutting

Rotary Cutter: Friend or Foe

A rotary cutter is wonderful and useful. When not used correctly, the sharp blade can be a dangerous tool. Follow these safety tips:

1. Never cut toward you.

2. Use a sharp blade. Pressing harder on a dull blade can cause the blade to jump the ruler and injure your fingers.

3. Always disengage the blade before the cutter leaves your hand, even if you intend to pick it up immediately.

Rotary cutters have been caught when lifting fabric, have fallen onto the floor and have cut fingers.

Basic Sewing

You now have precisely cut strips that are exactly the correct width. You are well on your way to blocks that fit together perfectly. Accurate sewing is the next important step.

Matching Edges:

1. Carefully line up the edges of your strips. Many times, if the underside is off a little, your seam will be off by $\frac{1}{8}$". This does not sound like much until you have 8 seams in a block, each off by $\frac{1}{8}$". Now your finished block is a whole inch wrong!

2. Pin the pieces together to prevent them shifting.

Seam Allowance:

I cannot stress enough the importance of accurate $\frac{1}{4}$" seams. All the quilts in this book are measured for $\frac{1}{4}$" seams unless otherwise indicated.

Most sewing machine manufacturers offer a Quarter-inch foot. A Quarter-inch foot is the most worthwhile investment you can make in your quilting.

Pressing:

I want to talk about pressing even before we get to sewing because proper pressing can make the difference between a quilt that wins a ribbon at the quilt show and one that does not.

Press, do NOT iron. What does that mean? Many of us want to move the iron back and forth along the seam. This "ironing" stretches the strip out of shape and creates errors that accumulate as the quilt is constructed. Believe it or not, there is a correct way to press your seams, and here it is:

1. Do NOT use steam with your iron. If you need a little water, spritz it on.

2. Place your fabric flat on the ironing board without opening the seam. Set a hot iron on the seam and count to 3. Lift the iron and move to the next position along the seam. Repeat until the entire seam is pressed. This sets and sinks the threads into the fabric.

3. Now, carefully lift the top strip and fold it away from you so the seam is on one side. Usually the seam is pressed toward the darker fabric, but often the direction of the seam is determined by the piecing requirements.

4. Press the seam open with your fingers. Add a little water or spray starch if it wants to close again. Lift the iron and place it on the seam. Count to 3. Lift the iron again and continue until the seam is pressed. Do NOT use the tip of the iron to push the seam open. So many people do this and wonder later why their blocks are not fitting together.

5. Most critical of all: For accuracy every seam must be pressed before the next seam is sewn.

Working with 'Crosswise Grain' Strips:

Strips cut on the crosswise grain (from selvage to selvage) have problems similar to bias edges and are prone to stretching. To reduce stretching and make your quilt lay flat for quilting, keep these tips in mind.

1. Take care not to stretch the strips as you sew.

2. Adjust the sewing thread tension and the presser foot pressure if needed.

3. If you detect any puckering as you go, rip out the seam and sew it again. It is much easier to take out a seam now than to do it after the block is sewn.

Sewing Bias Edges:

Bias edges wiggle and stretch out of shape very easily. They are not recommended for beginners, but even a novice can accomplish bias edges if these techniques are employed.

1. Stabilize the bias edge with one of these methods:

a) Press with spray starch.

b) Press freezer paper or removable iron-on stabilizer to the back of the fabric.

c) Sew a double row of stay stitches along the bias edge and $\frac{1}{8}$" from the bias edge. This is a favorite technique of garment makers.

2. Pin, pin, pin! I know many of us dislike pinning, but when working with bias edges, pinning makes the difference between intersections that match and those that do not.

Building Better Borders:

Wiggly borders make a quilt very difficult to finish. However, wiggly borders can be avoided with these techniques.

1. Cut the borders on grain. That means cutting your strips parallel to the selvage edge.

2. Accurately cut your borders to the exact measure of the quilt.

3. If your borders are piece stripped from crosswise grain fabrics, press well with spray starch and sew a double row of stay stitches along the outside edge to maintain the original shape and prevent stretching.

4. Pin the border to the quilt, taking care not to stretch the quilt top to make it fit. Pinning reduces slipping and stretching.

Embroidery   Use 24" lengths of doubled pearl cotton or 6-ply floss and a #22 or #24 Chenille needle (this needle has a large eye). Outline large elements.

Running Stitch   Come up at A. Weave the needle through the fabric, making LONG stitches on the top and SHORT stitches on the bottom. Keep stitches even.

Applique Instructions

Basic Turned Edge

1. Trace pattern onto no-melt template plastic (or onto Wash-Away Tear-Away Stabilizer).

2. Cut out the fabric shape leaving a scant $\frac{1}{4}$" fabric border all around and clip the curves.

3. **Plastic Template Method** - Place plastic shape on the wrong side of the fabric. Spray edges with starch. Press a $\frac{1}{4}$" border over the edge of the template plastic with the tip of a hot iron. Press firmly.

Stabilizer Method - Place stabilizer shape on the wrong side of the fabric. Use a glue stick to press a $\frac{1}{4}$" border over the edge of the stabilizer securing it with the glue stick. Press firmly.

5. Remove the template, maintaining the folded edge on the back of the fabric.

6. Position the shape on the quilt and Blindstitch in place.

Basic Turned Edge by Hand

1. Cut out the shape leaving a $\frac{1}{4}$" fabric border all around.

2. Baste the shapes to the quilt, keeping the basting stitches away from the edge of the fabric.

3. Begin with all areas that are under other layers and work to the topmost layer.

4. For an area no more than 2" ahead of where you are working, trim to $\frac{1}{8}$" and clip the curves.

5. Using the needle, roll the edge under and sew tiny Blindstitches to secure.

Using Fusible Web for Iron-on Applique:

1. Trace pattern onto Steam a Seam 2 fusible web.

2. Press the patterns onto the wrong side of fabric.

3. Cut out patterns exactly on the drawn line.

4. Score web paper with a pin, then remove the paper.

5. Position the fabric, fusible side down, on the quilt. Press with a hot iron following the fusible web manufacturer's instructions.

6. Stitch around the edge by hand.

Optional: Stabilize the wrong side of the fabric with your favorite stabilizer.

Use a size 80 machine embroidery needle. Fill the bobbin with lightweight basting thread and thread machine with machine embroidery thread that complements the color being appliqued.

Set your machine for a Zigzag stitch and adjust the thread tension if needed. Use a scrap to experiment with different stitch widths and lengths until you find the one you like best.

Sew slowly.

Basic Layering Instructions

Marking Your Quilt:

If you choose to mark your quilt for hand or machine quilting, it is much easier to do so before layering. Press your quilt before you begin. Here are some handy tips regarding marking.

1. A disappearing pen may vanish before you finish.

2. Use a White pencil on dark fabrics.

3. If using a washable Blue pen, remember that pressing may make the pen permanent.

Pieced Backings:

1. Press the backing fabric before measuring.

2. If possible cut backing fabrics on grain, parallel to the selvage edges.

3. Piece 3 parts rather than 2 whenever possible, sewing 2 side borders to the center. This reduces stress on the pieced seam.

4. Backing and batting should extend at least 2" on each side of the quilt.

Creating a Quilt Sandwich:

1. Press the backing and top to remove all wrinkles.

2. Lay the backing wrong side up on the table.

3. Position the batting over the backing and smooth out all wrinkles.

4. Center the quilt top over the batting leaving a 2" border all around.

5. Pin the layers together with 2" safety pins positioned a handwidth apart. A grapefruit spoon makes inserting the pins easier. Leaving the pins open in the container speeds up the basting on the next quilt.

Basic Quilting Instructions

Hand Quilting:

Many quilters enjoy the serenity of hand quilting. Because the quilt is handled a great deal, it is important to securely baste the sandwich together. Place the quilt in a hoop and don't forget to hide your knots.

Machine Quilting:

All the quilts in this book were machine quilted. Some were quilted on a large, free-arm quilting machine and others were quilted on a sewing machine. If you have never machine quilted before, practice on some scraps first.

Straight Line Machine Quilting Tips:

1. Pin baste the layers securely.

2. Set up your sewing machine with a size 80 quilting needle and a walking foot.

3. Experimenting with the decorative stitches on your machine adds interest to your quilt. You do not have to quilt the entire piece with the same stitch. Variety is the spice of life, so have fun trying out stitches you have never used before as well as your favorite stand-bys.

Free Motion Machine Quilting Tips:

1. Pin baste the layers securely.

2. Set up your sewing machine with a spring needle, a quilting foot, and lower the feed dogs.

Basic Mitered Binding

A Perfect Finish:

The binding endures the most stress on a quilt and is usually the first thing to wear out. For this reason, we recommend using a double fold binding.

1. Trim the backing and batting even with the quilt edge.

2. If possible cut strips on the crosswise grain because a little bias in the binding is a Good thing. This is the only place in the quilt where bias is helpful, for it allows the binding to give as it is turned to the back and sewn in place.

3. Strips are usually cut 2½" wide, but check the instructions for your project before cutting.

4. Sew strips end to end to make a long strip sufficient to go all around the quilt plus 4"- 6".

5. With wrong sides together, fold the strip in half lengthwise. Press.

6. Stretch out your hand and place your little finger at the corner of the quilt top. Place the binding where your thumb touches the edge of the quilt. Aligning the edge of the quilt with the raw edges of the binding, pin the binding in place along the first side.

7. Leaving a 2" tail for later use, begin sewing the binding to the quilt with a ¼" seam.

For Mitered Corners:

1. Stop ¼" from the first corner. Leave the needle in the quilt and turn it 90°. Hit the reverse button on your machine and back off the quilt leaving the threads connected.

2. Fold the binding perpendicular to the side you sewed, making a 45° angle. Carefully maintaining the first fold, bring the binding back along the edge to be sewn.

3. Carefully align the edges of the binding with the quilt edge and sew as you did the first side. Repeat this process until you reach the tail left at the beginning. Fold the tail out of the way and sew until you are ¼" from the beginning stitches.

4. Remove the quilt from the machine. Fold the quilt out of the way and match the binding tails together. Carefully sew the binding tails with a ¼" seam. You can do this by hand if you prefer.

Finishing the Binding:

5. Trim the seam to reduce bulk.

6. Finish stitching the binding to the quilt across the join you just sewed.

7. Turn the binding to the back of the quilt. To reduce bulk at the corners, fold the miter in the opposite direction from which it was folded on the front.

8. Hand-sew a Blind stitch on the back of the quilt to secure the binding in place.

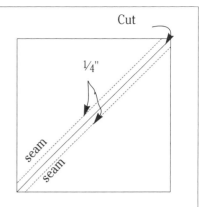

Half-Square Triangle
1. Place 2 squares right sides together.
2. Draw a diagonal line from corner to corner.
3. Stitch ¼" on each side of the line.
4. Cut squares apart on the diagonal line.
5. Open the 2 new squares with 2 colors.
6. Press. Trim off dog-ears.
7. Center and trim to size.

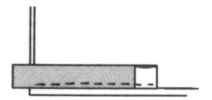

Align the raw edge of the binding with the raw edge of the quilt top. Start about 8" from the corner and go along the first side with a ¼" seam.

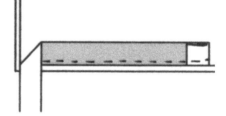

Stop ¼" from the edge. Then stitch a slant to the corner (through both layers of binding)... lift up, then down, as you line up the edge. Fold the binding back.

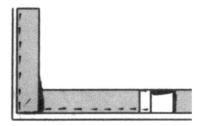

Align the raw edge again. Continue stitching the next side with a ¼" seam as you sew the binding in place.

Upstairs and Downstairs

photos on pages 50 - 51
SIZE: 52" x 76"
YARDAGE:
We used a *Moda* "Rouenneries" by French General
'Jelly Roll' collection of $2\frac{1}{2}$" strips
- we purchased 1 'Jelly Roll'

8 strips	OR	$\frac{5}{8}$ yard Medium Gray
7 strips	OR	$\frac{1}{2}$ yard Light Gray
5 strips	OR	$\frac{3}{8}$ yard Faded Red
5 strips	OR	$\frac{3}{8}$ yard Cream
3 strips	OR	$\frac{1}{4}$ yard Red

Border #2   Purchase $\frac{1}{2}$ yard Gray/Red print
Blocks, Border #3 & Binding Purchase 2 yards Red print
Backing   Purchase $3\frac{3}{8}$ yards
Batting   Purchase 60" x 84"
Sewing machine, needle, thread

PREPARATION FOR SQUARES:
Cut all strips $2\frac{1}{2}$" x width of fabric (usually 42" - 44").
Label the stacks or pieces as you cut.

SORTING:
Sort the following strips:

position	quantity	color
Blocks	8	Medium Gray
	7	Light Gray
	5	Cream
	3	Red
Border #1	5	Faded Red

CUTTING:
Refer to the Cutting chart. Label pieces as you cut.

CUTTING CHART

color	quantity	length	position

Yardage:

Red print	15	$6\frac{1}{2}$" x $6\frac{1}{2}$"	#1

NOTE: Cut $6\frac{1}{2}$" x $6\frac{1}{2}$" pieces parallel to the selvage to
provide fabric piece for Border #3.
Jelly Roll Strips:

Red	45	$2\frac{1}{2}$"	#3, 6, 9
Cream	30	$6\frac{1}{2}$"	#2, 4
Light Gray	30	$8\frac{1}{2}$"	#5, 7
Medium Gray	30	$10\frac{1}{2}$"	#8, 10

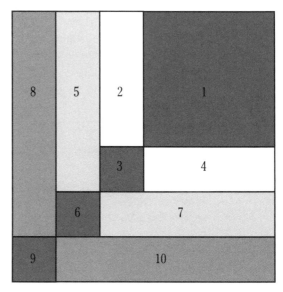

Block Assembly Diagram

MAKING THE BLOCKS:
Sew #2 to the left side of #1. Press.
Sew #3 to #4. Press.
Sew #3-4 to the bottom of #1-2. Press.
Sew #5 to the left side of the piece. Press.
Sew #6 to #7. Press.
Sew #6-7 to the bottom of the piece. Press.
Sew #8 to the left side of the piece. Press.
Sew #9 to #10. Press.
Sew #9-10 to the bottom of the piece. Press.

Make a total of 15 blocks.
Each block will measure $12\frac{1}{2}$" x $12\frac{1}{2}$" at this point.

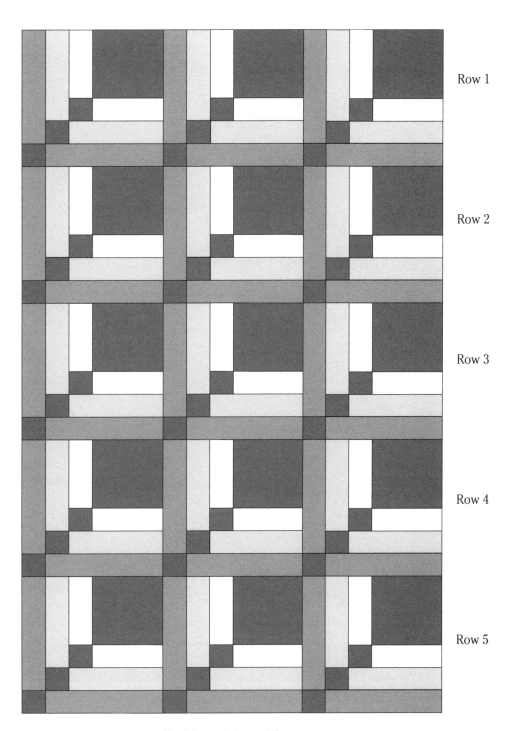

Row 1

Row 2

Row 3

Row 4

Row 5

Upstairs and Downstairs
Quilt Assembly Diagram

ASSEMBLY:
Arrange all blocks on a work surface or table.
Sew blocks together in 5 rows,
3 blocks per row.
Press.
Sew the rows together.
Press.

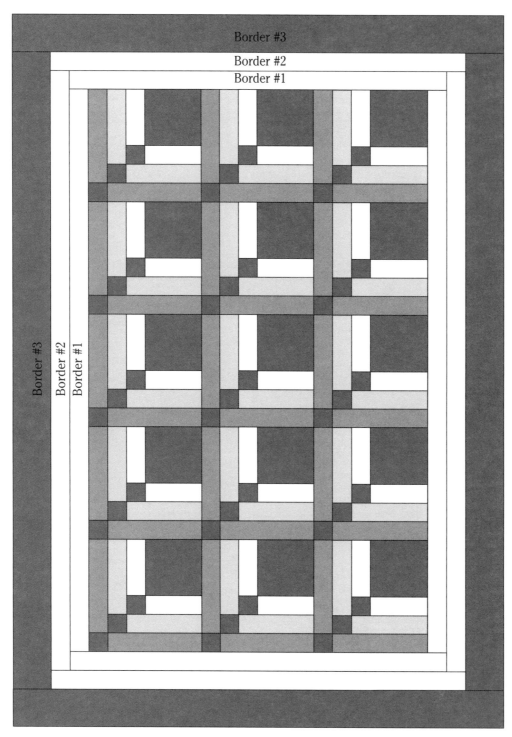

Border #3

Border #2

Border #1

Border #3

Border #2

Border #1

Upstairs and Downstairs
Quilt Assembly Diagram

BORDERS:
Border #1:
 Sew Faded Red strips end to end.
 Cut 2 strips $2\frac{1}{2}$" x $60\frac{1}{2}$" for sides.
 Cut 2 strips $2\frac{1}{2}$" x $40\frac{1}{2}$" for top and bottom.
 Sew side borders to the quilt. Press.
 Sew top and bottom borders to the quilt. Press.

Border #2:
 Cut 2 strips $2\frac{1}{2}$" x $64\frac{1}{2}$" for sides.
 Cut 2 strips $2\frac{1}{2}$" x $44\frac{1}{2}$" for top and bottom.
 Sew side borders to the quilt. Press.
 Sew top and bottom borders to the quilt. Press.

Outer Border #3:
Cut strips $4\frac{1}{2}$" wide parallel to the selvage to
  eliminate piecing.
 Cut 2 strips $4\frac{1}{2}$" x $68\frac{1}{2}$" for sides.
 Cut 2 strips $4\frac{1}{2}$" x $52\frac{1}{2}$" for top and bottom.
 Sew side borders to the quilt. Press.
 Sew top and bottom borders to the quilt. Press.

FINISHING:
Quilting: See Basic Instructions.
Binding: Cut strips $2\frac{1}{2}$" wide.
  Sew together end to end to equal 266".
  See Binding Instructions.

Along the Lane

photos on page 43
SIZE: 59" x 75½"

YARDAGE:
We used a *Moda* "Essence" by Sandy Gervais
    'Dessert Roll' collection of 5" x 44" fabric strips
    - we purchased 1 'Dessert Roll'

2 strips	OR	⅓ yard Brown
2 strips	OR	⅓ yard Red
2 strips	OR	⅓ yard Green
2 strips	OR	⅓ yard Tan
2 strips	OR	⅓ yard Burgundy

Alternate Strip   Purchase 1⅓ yards Green floral print
Border #1   Purchase ¼ yard Burgundy print
Border #2 & Binding   Purchase 1⅞ yard Green print
Backing   Purchase 3¾ yards
Batting   Purchase 67" x 84"
Sewing machine, needle, thread

PREPARATION FOR STRIPS:
Cut all strips 5" x width of fabric (usually 42" - 44").

CUTTING:
From Green floral print yardage, cut 5 strips parallel
    to the selvage 5" x 45½".

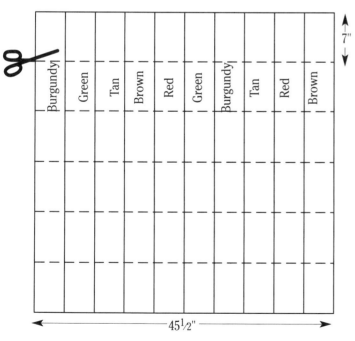

Strip Sets

STRIP SETS:
Sew the following 5" strips together:
    Burgundy-Green-Tan-Brown-Red-Green-Burgundy-Tan-Red-Brown
            to make a piece 42" x 45½". Press.
    Cut 6 sections, each 7" x 45½".

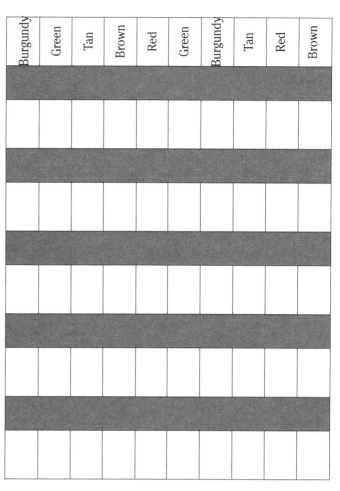

Along the Lane
Quilt Assembly Diagram

ASSEMBLY:
Arrange all blocks on a work surface or table.
Alternate 7" x 45½" strip sets with the
    5" x 45½" Green print strips.
On alternate strip set rows, flip the strip set to
    change the order of the colors.
Sew the rows together.
    Press.

Along the Lane
Quilt Assembly Diagram

BORDERS:
Border #1:
Cut 2 strips $1\frac{1}{2}$" x 62" for sides.
Cut 2 strips $1\frac{1}{2}$" x $47\frac{1}{2}$" for top and bottom.
Sew side borders to the quilt. Press.
Sew top and bottom borders to the quilt. Press.

Outer Border #2:
Cut strips $6\frac{1}{2}$" wide parallel to the selvage to
    eliminate piecing.
Cut 2 strips $6\frac{1}{2}$" x 64" for sides.
Cut 2 strips $6\frac{1}{2}$" x $59\frac{1}{2}$" for top and bottom.
Sew side borders to the quilt. Press.
Sew top and bottom borders to the quilt. Press.

FINISHING:
Quilting:
    See Basic Instructions.

Binding:
    Cut strips $2\frac{1}{2}$" wide.
    Sew together end to end to equal 279".
    See Binding Instructions.

Along the Lane

pieced by Donna Arends Hansen
quilted by Julie Lawson

When it's time to use up your stash of leftover yardages, this design allows you to combine that pretty print with an assortment of 5" strips for a fast and easy quilt that is simply irresistible.

This quilt is amazingly simple and fast to make.

instructions on pages 41 - 42

"Essence" by Sandy Gervais 'Dessert Roll' 5" strips

Peaches and Cream

pieced by Edna Summers
quilted by Sue Needle

Capture the romance of the 18th and 19th centuries and quilt a new piece of history for your home with these reproduction fabrics.

Red, tan, light cream and peach combine with gentle finesse in subtle scale patterns that will blend comfortably with even the most modern decor.

instructions on pages 25 - 27

"Aster Manor" by 3 Sisters 'Dessert Roll' 5" strips

Stair Steps to Heaven

pieced by Rose Ann Pegram
quilted by Sue Needle

Sumptuous colors and pretty prints with plenty of variety coordinate beautifully with any decor.

This fast and fabulous quilt will soon become a family favorite. Remember this one next time you need a quick gift idea for someone special.

instructions on pages 28 - 29

"Aster Manor" by 3 Sisters 'Layer Cake' 10" squares

Steps Around the World

pieced by Donna Perrotta
quilted by Julie Lawson

Earth and Sky entwine in resplendent tones shaping the harmony of Mother Nature in a comfortable, cozy quilt. These rich colors are especially appealing to the men in your family.

Perfect for the fireside reading chair, den, or family room - more often than not - you may also find this quilt on your son's bed. It's so quick and easy, you might want to make two!

instructions on pages 30 - 33

"Alliance" by Howard Marcus 'Layer Cake' 10" squares